Untitled – Graphite on Paper, Harijs Grauds c1950

Boys of the Dvina

3rd Edition,

Printed by Lulu Publishing in the USA and Canada

ISBN: 978-1-300-01591-8

Boys of the Dvina

Latvia's Army 1918-1940

To my Grandfather, Harijs

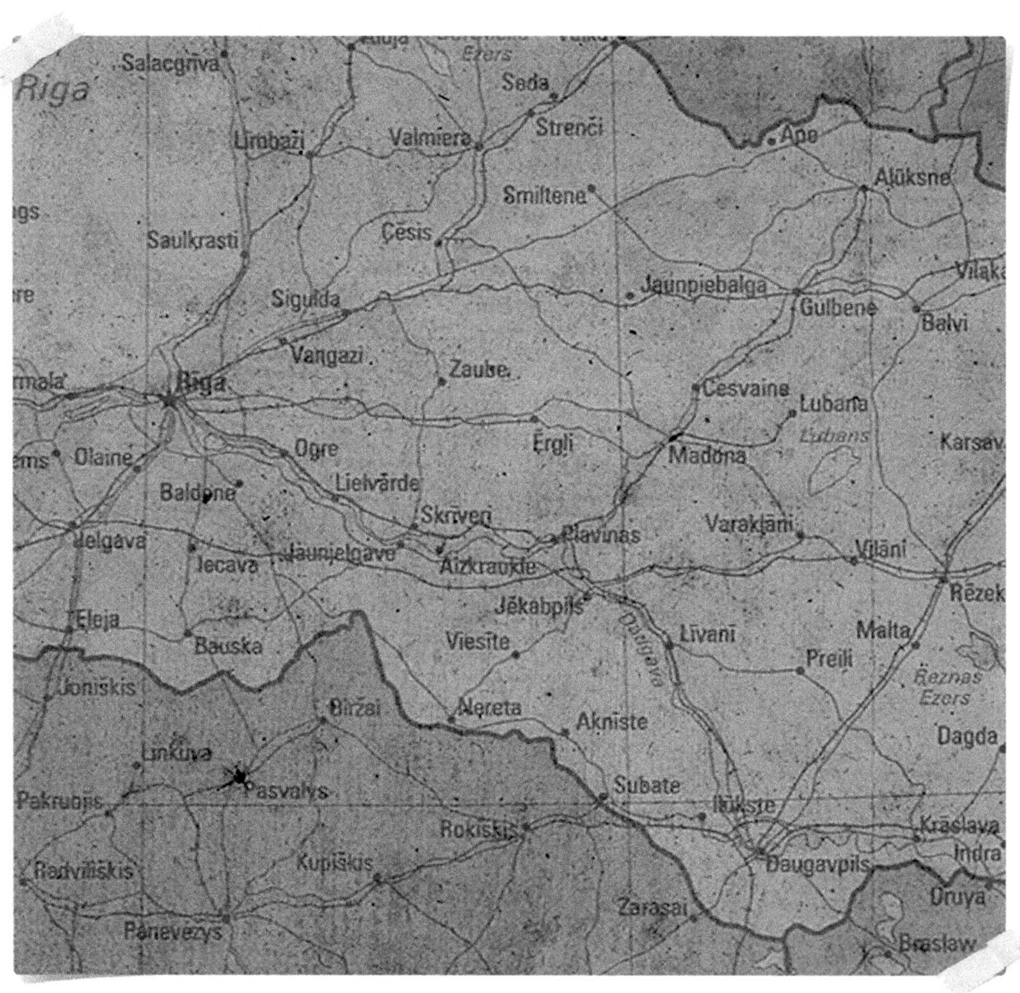

Salacgrīva
Riga
Seda
Strenči
Limbaži
Valmiera
Ape
Alūksne
Smiltene
Saulkrasti
Cēsis
Jaunpiebalga
Gulbene
Balvi
Sigulda
Vangazi
Zaube
Rīga
Cesvaine
Lubāna
Lubāns
Olaine
Ogre
Ērgli
Madona
Baldone
Lielvārde
Skrīveri
Pļaviņas
Varakļāni
Jelgava
Iecava
Jaunjelgava
Aizkraukle
Viļāni
Jēkabpils
Eleja
Bauska
Viesīte
Daugava
Līvāni
Malta
Preiļi
Rēznas Ezers
Joniškis
Biržai
Nereta
Akniste
Dagda
Linkuva
Pasvalys
Subate
Pakruojis
Ilūkste
Krāslava
Rokiškis
Indra
Radviliškis
Kupiškis
Daugavpils
Druya
Zarasai
Panevezys
Braslaw

Preface to the Third Edition

A number of years ago I found myself in possession of a few dozen photos of Latvian soldiers from the period between World War I and World War II. The men were dressed sharp and frozen in time; they were unaware of the terrible fate that, in only a few years, would befall themselves, their families, and their country. These men, ready to fight, would be ordered to put down their arms and surrender to the Soviet Union. Many would pay dearly for this mistake, many would flee to the woods to become partisans, known as "Forest Brothers" to continue resistance even though the leaders of their country did not want them to fight, or in any case, saw it as futile against the Soviet bohemoth.

The third edition expands on previous work, adding new information, new sections, many new pictures some of which were taken by myself on my trip to Riga in 2001 and some of which were given to me by family who had taken them on previous trips. As I stated in the second edition, I am pleased, even thrilled, to share the results of this research with the few that are interested in this niche topic. I do believe that this is still the only English volume on the Latvian Army of the Independence period, but interest is growing. A trilingual book was published recently about one small detail of the Latvian Army uniform, thus there must be some enthusiasm for Latvian history in the English speaking world. As Eastern Europe begins to open up, I see more and more photos of Latvian Army soldiers on auction sites, waiting to be explained and decoded. I hope to help some interested individuals understand the hidden history in these photos, and satisfy the same urge to uncover the past that motivated me to write this small tribute.

Illustration 1: Karlis Grauds, my great-grandfather. A tailor in the Latvian Army and later a soldier in the Latvian Legion.

Table of Contents

Salacgriva
Riga
Seda
Strenči
Limbaži
Valmiera
Ape
Alūksne
Smiltene
Saulkrasti
Subate
Ilūkste
Rokiškis
Daugavpils
Kupiškis
Radviliškis
Zarasai
Panevezys
Druya
Braslaw

Introduction

The Great War, that is to say the First World War, was *the* defining experience of modernity; it was the catalyst for revolutions in art, science, war, and in the political discourse and structure of Europe. It was the Great War that would return the world to mass slaughter in 1939, the Great War that would set the conditions for ethnic division and social strife, and the Great War that would bring to an end the vast Slavic empire, Imperial Russia, in 1917. The war was Great in every sense of such an ambiguous term - it was, among many things, both terrible and rife with great opportunity.

From the ruin of the former tsardom in the East, Imperial Russia, new nation-states were born that had never existed before in history.

Illustration 2: In a photo dated 23 May, 1933, two soldiers pose on the banks of the Lielupe river. They are likely infantry soldiers from the 3rd Jelgava Regiment.

Latvia, Lithuania, Estonia, and Finland are only some of the states who owed their birth or rebirth, at least in part, to the violent end of an empire that had existed since 1721.

These new fledgling states had to create governments with nothing, from nothing. They had been ruthlessly suppressed and Russified during Imperial rule by authoritarians who wished to keep them segregated and uneducated. Nationalist movements, however, pushed back against the feudal lords in the 1905 Revolution and by 1917, national consciousness had become a *tour de force* that moved inexhorably toward the realization of new national governments.

These new governments would become unique and unusual blends between East and West, adopting the Western values of freedom and individual rights in a sea of influential states like Germany and Russia that traditionally valued obedience and subserviance to authority. In nations that oscillated from love to hatred of Russia, to the idolization of England,[1] it was an imperfect experiment, but one that ultimately showed the Western orientation of Russia's indo-European populations; a phenomenon that had developed under unlikely circumstances.[2]

After the Great War, Latvia, Lithuania, and Estonia only existed for a short period before their independence was snuffed out by the imperial ambitions of the Soviet Union and Nazi Germany; Latvia did not resist like Finland did and never got to put its army to the test, but Latvia's existence during this moment in history was important. It established the cultural value-base which would motivate the peoples of this small state to strive for freedom, forge the living memory of a time of independence, and form a mission for a future rebirth of national existence.

---

1 Even after World War II, a partisan group opposing Soviet occupation dubbed itself "The First English Regiment."

2 Latvia's true democratic period ended in 1934 under Karlis Ulmanis who formed a Liberal dictatorship rationalized by the threat of Communist insurgents. During this time, the constitution was to be amended to resemble more the American model which protected property rights from Socialist movements.

This snapshot in the history of Latvia is of interest because it illustrates a unique pheonenon not seen elsewhere in modern Europe. It is the creation of a nation and its army from nothing, the fusion of diverse traditions, and the ambitions of a small people to finally emerge from the darkness of the Russian winter and claim their own place in the sun.

Illustration 3: New recruits leave for basic military training, 12 April 1937. All Latvian men were required to serve in the armed forces when they turned 21.

I originally did not intend this publication to be the definitive volume on the Latvian army between the wars, but over the past year it has broadened and become more detailed than before. I still do, however, approach this subject with humility and stress that my research, like any research, is always incomplete. I hope to make claims in this book which can be corrected and amended by experts on the topic (if any exist) and to motivate further research in English about Latvia's great experiment in the creation of a military and national culture from nothing more than its social memory and the ruin of its old imperial masters.

One final note on the title. In Europe, there are as many names for places as there are people, cultures, and local dialects. Daugavpils, for instance, a town on Latvia's southeastern frontier, is known as Dunaberg in German, Dyneberg in Polish and Yiddish, Daugpils in Latgallian, and Dvinsk in Russian. Thus one might justifiably wonder why I've chosen the title *Boys of the Dvina* rather than *Boys of the Daugava,* the traditional Baltic name for the river that bifurcates Latvia. The title is meant to be a tounge-in-cheek reference to the way Latvia's former ruler, Imperial Russia, viewed the upstart army. Latvian soldiers were merely young men from the far Western reaches of what the dynastic clan saw as "Russia"; the army was formed, in the crucible of the Great War, from boys of the Tsar's dominion of the Western Dvina, a force simultaneously both greatly valued and greatly underestimated by him; the boys from the Dvina were, in the end, the force that helped defeat the most formidable empire in Europe.

S. Kiersons, 2013

"...The streams in the valleys flowed red with blood
As chains of slavery held Kurland's nation
Her warriors all slain by a cruel invader.
Soon, soon the castle of light sunk in the mountain.
There sleep the ancient Gods of the nation,
There sleep the cultural treasures of the fatherland.
If the secret password is remembered, the castle will rise again.
The glory of our nation's past will send gold rays worldwide.
The sons of the nation recalled the long forgotten treasure,
They called for light, light dawned anew,
And the castle of light rose from the mountain!..."

- Castle of Light, Auseklis (1850-1879)

I – History

Nothing in history emerges without some kind of liniage, and although the Latvian army appeared in full form in the 1920s where it had never existed before, it had in fact been formed in its infancy by Latvia's perceived national enemy – Russia.

It was combat, rather than any nationalistic campaign by political activists or intellectuals, that formed the core of Latvia's sense of unity in mission. Latvia was devastated by the war, both at the front and at home, losing 25% of its population – more by percentage than any country in the war - and its young men were united in combat against German aggression in the East. From 1917 the Eastern Front bifurcated the country, running through Latvia's towns and villages.

This unintended forging of national identities was not unique, and in fact Latvia was not the only national consciousness thought to have been cast from the crucible of the Great War. It was the common experience of the nascent cultures of Canada, India, and also other peoples of the Russian empire.

Illustration 4: Latvian Riflemen in the trenches during the pivotal Christmas Battles of 1916.

It was partly convenience that made the accidental formation of the core of national armies possible. In Latvia as in

Canada it was thought to be good for morale, communication, and administration to divide the colonials into ethnic regiments within a larger imperial army. In Russia, no local units recruited from a single area were permitted[3] – but Latvia became an exception when in 1915, under the duress of invading German troops, Nicholas II hesitently authorized an ethnic Latvian division.

Thus Latvian units began to look and act distinct already in the First World War. The 5th Zemgale Regiment had its own badges, Latvian language, and even a flag. The flag bore the motto: "The Freedom of our Fatherland we will purchase with our blood." Although this kind of dual-meaning rose the eyebrow of a few in the Russian officer corps, the regiment was allowed these priveledges by Nicholas II. The Tsar, like Joseph Stalin in the Second World War, was willing to make ideological sacrifices for the sake of utilitarian results; and patriotism was an undeniable component of an army's morale.

Illustration 5: 5th Zemgale Regiment Flag with founding date 1915.

The intended consequence of this division was success on the battlefield. The Latvian Riflemen, eight regiments of elite troops, were recognized as some of Imperial Russia's most valuable soldiers, and ironically became Vladimir Lenin's elite guard - the key to the success of the Revolution in 1917. Jukums Vācietis, a Colonel in the Latvian Riflemen, would go on to be the first Commander-in-Chief of the Soviet Russian Red Army.

3 This served dual purposes. While mixing all ethnicities within combat units allowed the administration to forestall nationalistic unity and promote loyalty to the empire instead, it also ensured that no single locality of the empire lost all of its young men in battle.

The unintended consequence of this division was that victories and defeats shared among national groups created sharp contrasts in perception when soldiers became disenchanted with their superiors. The Riflemen's motto "A Free Latvia within a Free Russia" became more chimerical and national autonomy no longer seemed satisfactory. Virtually all armies in the Great War experienced mass mutiny at about the point where the number of casualties equalled total mobilized strength. In Russia and other empires, mutiny would inevitably rail against the foreign "other" as the nationalist perception became augmented by this fact of administrative division. After the Christmas Battles and the attendant losses in 1916- 1917 matters became somewhat more tense between the troops, their Latvian commanders, and the Tsarist Regime. Bolshevist ideas that proffered an immediate end to the war and the oppression of the Russian Empire began to resonate. By the time of the revolution, 25 000 Riflemen had been demobilized and about 77% of the officer corps had joined the Whites in the Russian Revolution and Civil War. In contrast to the significance placed upon them by Soviet historians, only about 12 000 Latvian Riflemen had become "Red Latvian Riflemen," leaving the rest to form the core of the Latvian national army. The Red Riflemen, while instrumental to the success of Bolshevik forces in Russia, were only a small contingent of elite Latvian shock troops. After the Soviet occupation of Latvia beginning in 1944, the Red Riflemen would be used to show that Latvians were true communists and thus legitimize the

Illustration 6: After the Germans marched into Latvia in 1917, this medallion was minted with the inscription "On 3 September 1917 Riga was Freed."

occupation of their country by Soviet Russia.

The inward focus of Russia during the October Revolution and ensuing civil war ultimately meant that German forces came to dominate in Latvia at the end of the Great War. Immediately after the 1917 revolution and withdrawl of Russian forces into the chaos of the motherland, Germany, who had already negotiated peace with Russia, occupied virtually all of Latvia, proclaiming to the world that they had "freed" it, but after their unconditional surrender to the remaining Entente nations in November 1918, Latvia became entrenched in what was in fact a civil war with Latvians and foreigners on all sides.

On the 18th of November, the liberal Republic of Latvia was formed under President Kārlis Ulmanis. By December, the Latvian Red Army, backed by Soviet Russia and the communist government of Pēteris Stučka, invaded the territory of Latvia proper. The Latvian communists commanded Russia's most effective shock troops – the Red Latvian Riflemen. Stučka and Ulmanis would become leaders of movements with opposing ideals for the future of Latvia. To complicate the chaotic nature of the civil war, the Baltic *Landswehr*, a German *Freikorps* force once called the "vanguard of Nazism," would attempt to secure Latvia for the German barons under the title of the United Baltic Duchy. The result was a three-way tug of war that would end in ruin for two parties.

Illustration 7: Kārlis Ulmanis, leader of the liberal democratic forces during the Independence War, passes by supporters in 1934 as the President of the Republic of Latvia. They give him the Roman salute, likely inspired by the Latvia's close relationship with Italy at the time.

The Red Army initially took nearly all of Latvia without

resistance leaving Ulmanis' government only a small pocket of territory around Liepāja (Libau). Stučka's government, now ruling in the capital Riga, immediately began to bring the revolution home, instituting sweeping socialist reforms intended to bring about the dictatorship of the proletariat. In Russia proper, the revolution was seen as pre-mature – Russia had little industry. In Latvia, with the most developed working class in all of Russia, it was recognized that the country would become a true experiment in socialism - a nation ripe for a workers' revolution.

The effects were devastating. After the popular wresting of land from the "bourgeoisie" (actually the nobility), the regime's base of support declined meteorically. Farmers refused to supply the cities with

Illustration 8: A rag-tag section of early Latvian Army soldiers from 6 Regiment Riga. Circa 1920, all wear mixed uniforms,some with Latvian markings

food because they were now being enslaved in the name of the "people" as opposed to the nobility. As shortages in the cities abounded, the only effective response was to launch a wave of terror. Revolutionary Tribunals ran show trials to execute "counter-revolutionaries" and deter farmers who felt they were being indentured to a new master instead of being aided in their promised liberation.

Illustration 9: The Bretheren Cemetary, Riga. A place of honor for Latvia's war dead, the cemetary is home to many soldiers who gave their lives for Latvian independence. Many grave markers have no name.

The communist reign was short-lived, and a few months after the conquering of Latvia by the Red Army, the liberal regime under Ulmanis counter-attacked with the support of German Baltic *Landswehr* forces on the 3rd of March 1919. The counter-attack left Red Army forces reeling and Riga was recaptured on the 22nd of May, 1919. Stučka's communist government was now left with only with a part of the eastern province of Latgale which it ruled until combined Latvian and Polish forces pushed the communists back into Russia in 1920.

But the struggle was not over. Ulmanis' supposed allies, the aforementioned *Freikorps*, under the United Baltic Duchy, had launched a *coup d'etat* against him and as a final act of trechery prepared an attack on the capital Riga, in order to claim Latvia for the Baltic Nobility. A hastily assembled rag-tag Latvian army dug in and fought the final Battle of Riga, not against the Red Army this time, but against the Russian-led "West Russian Volunteer Army," composed mainly of Germans wishing to restore their dominance in the region. In an amazing instance of *deus ex machina,* the British Royal Navy coordinated an artillery attack from sea and supplied arms to the Latvians at this crucial moment – an act that would heavily influence the future outlook of the newborn nation.

The "Russian" army was defeated and chased westward out of Latvia. During the final stage, Latvian liberal forces turned eastward and pushed the Red Army out of Latgale; Ulmanis' government was finally victorious with the signing of the Latvian-Soviet treaty that same year. Casualties for the War of Independence amounted to over 10% of the army on the Latvian side with over 3 000 dead and 4 000 wounded. Although the ultimate price was paid by these soldiers, the casualties of the Independence War were almost miniscule in a nation that had lost over 700 000 men in the Great War.

Illustration 10: The Liberation War was the central myth of the Latvian army and the nation as a whole. Pictured here is one of the monuments that survived Soviet occupation. Photographed in 1991, this monument is situated near Litene.

The Independence War became the uniting myth of the Latvian nation. Even its flag was conceived in the ranks of the army in a war that symbolized the sacrifice ordinary people would undergo to acheive freedom. The only test of the Latvian army's combat abilities was in this very war, and in the end, a hastily assembled force defeated two stronger armies representing interests that had historically dominated the region. The Latvian army fulfilled the prophecy made by the national myth of *The Bear-Slayer* as Latvia finally cast off the yoke of the German nobility and the Russian empire in one war.

The Latvian Army in Numbers

(at the Outset of 1920)

Soldiers	69 232
Machine Guns	271
Light Machine Guns	321
Artillery Pieces (Light, Med)	54
Mortars	33

A Latvian Soldier's Song

This song's lyrics led to it being sung not only in the First World War but throughout and well after the Second. It seems to foreshadow the Great War leading to Latvia's indepdendence.

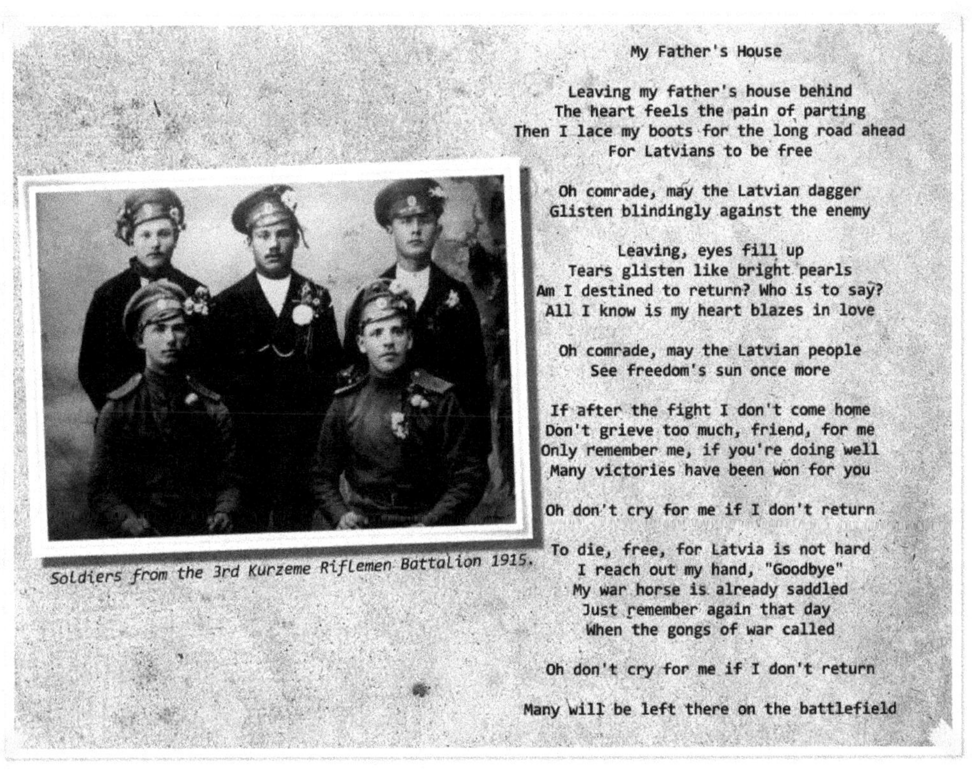

Soldiers from the 3rd Kurzeme Riflemen Battalion 1915.

"The soldiers are worried, the dawn breaks blood-red.
Do not worry brave soldiers, the sun will rise silver-white.
The snow fell, the wind howled, brave rode the cavalry.
They rode fast, I watched my dear brother ride along too.
They rode in the land, far and cruel; the land hostile, strange, and cold.
When the fatherland calls, when it suffers, its sons never hesitate.
The freedom of the fatherland they will purchase with their blood.
The love for their fatherland they showed with their deeds."

- A Song of the Latvian Riflemen

II - The Early Days

Latvia had a head-start in forming its own national army. Imperial Russia had put the machinery in place during the war when it began to allow the formation of distinct ethnic Latvian units. Although Tsar Nicholas II had some inkling of the danger of this action, essentially creating a machine that needed only to be comandeered, he was rightly convinced that even a united Latvia only strove for autonomy, not independence. It would be the war itself - its mismanagement and the wilful disregard for soldiers' lives - that would harden Latvians against Russia and deal the final blow to the empire. The war turned protests for autonomy into a bloody fight for independence.

After Russian withdrawal, the troops that were left behind or recruited in Latvia were a varied bunch. In the earliest days, that is the

Illustration 11: An early photo of Latvian soldiers wearing a variety of uniforms. Note the World War I signature "puttees" wrapped around some of the soldiers' legs.

days of the Northern and Southern Latvian Armies, equipment was scarce and diverse. Some soldiers had volunteered barefoot, with civilian clothing, but nonetheless just as ready to fight as their uniformed comrades-in-arms. Weapons and ammunition were of Russian and German manufacture, as well as uniforms when available. Britain had also supplied Latvians with uniforms and boots, sending enough supplies for 30 000 soldiers in 1919.

In a time of war, standardization of uniforms and equipment could not claim top priority, however standardization was and still is one of the key pillars of victory for any army. For Latvia, war was a logistical nightmare. Weapons used different ammunition, equipment all needed different replacement parts, and soldiers looked as if they had been assembled from the League of Nations. Although they had somehow managed to fight amidst all of this confusion, once the dust from the Independence War had settled, Latvia needed to devise standard equipment for the sake of logistics and combat effectiveness.

Illustration 12: A more defined Latvian look appeared in the 1920s. Pictured here is a platoon of Latvian soldiers from the 1st Infantry Regiment, Liepaja. NCOs and officers are in the center. The caps worn date this picture pre-1929.

Illustration 14: Two Soldiers with Family

Illustration 13: A Soldier from 8th Daugavpils Infantry Regiment

Illustration 15: Two enlisted men with stiff-peaked hats.10th Regiment Aizpute Marked Daugavpils 1928.

Illustration 16: An enlisted man posing with the soft-peaked cap (post 1929).

"The Latvian people on their father's shore
Still now no lords accept alone through birth;
They choose themselves their chiefs in times of war,
In peaceful times choose elders by their worth.
Well-known among the folk are those whose fame
Is earned through their great labours hard and long;
The people give them thanks and honoured name,
As heroes sing of them in sweetest song."

- The Bear-Slayer, Andrejs Pumpurs (1841-1902)

III – Organization

Like many small countries, Latvia felt the need to introduce universal conscription. This would mean that all Latvian males of serving age (21) would have military experience in the case of a national

Illustration 17: Troops execute "Eyes Right" command used for marching past senior officers. Latvia retained the Tsarist era Russian-style drill with bent elbows.

emergency. Obligatory service was for 10 months for infantry soldiers, and 12 months for all other branches. In 1940, the length of service for non-infantry trades was extended to 18 months. For career soldiers, a full career amounted to 29 years. Latvia also had reserve forces in which men 22-39 could serve. Older men could serve in the Home Guard (*Aizsargi*) from ages 40 to 50.

Illustration 18: A Lt.-Colonel Posed for a Photograph.

Peacetime troops in Latvia numbered 24 300 men, plus 1 200 in the Frontier Guard. Thus in peacetime, Latvia's troops amounted to about 1.24% of the total population. In a time of war it was estimated Latvia could raise an army of 150 000 men, which was realized only when Germany conscripted Latvians into the *Waffen SS* starting in 1943.

Just as in the United States, in war-time the President of the Republic was also the Commander-in-Chief of the military. Subordinated to the President was a military General, the Commander of the Latvian Army. The Minister of War handled the military budget. Directly subordinated to the Army Commander were the Division Commanders, including the commanders of Latvia's artillery, aviation, armor, navy, and cavarly units, all of whom had the rights of the main infantry division leaders.

Headquarters Battalion

The General Headquarters of the Latvian army (Staff Battalion) was comprised of General Headquarters itself, a Heavy Artillery Regiment, a Coastal Artillery Regiment, and an Armored Train

Illustration 19: This medical officer, a Captain, is pictured with HQ Battalion's signature light blue collar tabs.

Regiment (Latvia had 2 armored Trains).

The rest of the army was divided into 4 Divisions plus a Technical Division based in Riga. Each Infantry (*Kājnieki*) Division had a Division Headquarters, 3 Infantry Regiments, and an Artillery Regiment. The technical division of the Latvian military was comprised of a Division HQ, an Engineer (*Iženieris*) Regiment, a Tank (*Autotanku*) Regiment, a Signals (*Signālis*) Regiment, and an Aircraft (*Aviācija*) Regiment.

1st Infantry Division, Kurzeme

The 1st Kurzeme Infantry Division was established in mid-July 1919 after the Cesis Battles from the Southern Latvian Army. The first divisional commander was Jānis Balodis, a Colonel at the time, who later became Commander in Chief of the Latvian Army, a cabinet member, and vice president. From 1925 on, the division was commanded by a General. The division was headquartered in the city of Liepaja and comprised the 1st Liepaja Infantry Regiment, the 2nd Ventspils Infantry Regiment, the 3rd Jelgava Infantry Regiment, and the Kurzeme Artillery Regiment.

2nd Infantry Division, Vidzeme

The 2nd Division was also organized after the 1919 Cesis Battles but from the Northern Latvian Army. At first commanded by Colonel Mārtiņš Peniķis, a former officer in the Latvian Riflemen, the division was stationed in Riga. The 2nd Division encompassed the 4th Valmiera Infantry Regiment, the 5th Cesis Infantry Regiment, the 6th Riga Infantry Regiment, and the Vidzeme Artillery Regiment.

3rd Infantry Division, Latgale

Illustration 20: A Corporal from 3rd Infantry Division, 9 Rezekne Regiment.

The 3rd Latgale Division was based in Cesis. Its first commander was Krišjānis Berķis, former commander of 6th Tukums Regiment and one of the Latvian Riflemen officers who refused to join the Bolsheviks in 1917 and was arrested. Returning from Finland in 1919, he commanded the 3rd Division after the Cesis Battles. The 3rd Division participated in the Riga defence and liberation battles, going on to rid Latgale of Bolshevik forces. It was composed of the 7th Sigulda Infantry Regiment, the 8th Daugavpils Infantry Regiment, the 9th Rezekne Infantry Regiment, and the Latgale Artillery Regiment.

4th Infantry Division, Zemgale

Zemgale Division was formed in the battles of 1919 and took part in the push of Red forces out of Latgale. Commanded by a Baltic German Colonel, later General, Oskars Dankers. The 4th Division included the 10th Aizpute Infantry Regiment, the 11th Dobele Infantry Regiment, the 12th Bauska Infantry Regiment, and the Zemgale Artillery Regiment. Notably, the 4th Division also had Latvia's only Cavalry Regiment, the 1st Cavalry Regiment, located in historic Daugavpils Fortress, the former Western defensive base of the Russian empire.

Illustration 21: Latvian soldiers irreverently posing on obstacle course equipment.

Aviation Regiment

On June 7, 1919, during the height of the Independence War, the Latvian Aviation branch was established as a detachment. Latvian liberal-democratic forces effectively fought in the air. Fighter aces such as Lieutenant Peteris Tomsons was credited with 11 victories in 1919. In 1921, the detachment became a Division but in 1926 it was changed to a Regiment subordinated to the Technical Division in Riga. The Regiment was composed of 3 fighter squadrons, 4 land reconnaisance squadrons and a fleet recon squadron. Fleet recon pilots wore the Navy uniform while all other pilots wore the army Aviation Regiment uniform.

The whole regiment possessed under 150 planes. Bases were located in Riga, Ramava, Jumpravmuiza, Koknese, Gulbene, and Krustpils, but the main airbases were in Liepaja and Usma. Although Latvian units participated in no battles beyond the Independence War, many individual pilots would go on to fly for Germany and the Soviet Union as air aces in World War II. Both officers and non-comissioned ranks could become pilots.

Illustration 22: A postcard depicting world-famous Latvian aviator Herberts Cukurs circa 1933. Although he won international fame for Latvia in the interwar period, in World War II Cukurs became a leader of the infamous Arajs Kommando responsible for warcrimes in Latvia. He was assasinated by Mossad in 1965.

Illustration 23: Erected in 1939, the Armored Vehicle Brigade monument stresses the importance of armored cars to the victory of liberal democratic forces in the Independence War. It fell into disrepair during Soviet occupation.

Armored Vehicle Regiment

Also subordinated to the Technical Division in Riga, Latvia had one regiment of armored vehicles, including tanks. The Armored Vehicle Regiment (*Autotanku Pulks*) originated in the Independence War as a small car division belonging to Soviet forces. Upon withdrawal from Riga, much of their equipment was abandoned for lack of repairs, and armored cars including "Bearslayer" and "Imants" were taken over by the Baltic *Landswehr.* At first, the Armored Vehicle Division contained armored trains and cars, both of which participated in curcial ways during the battles in Latgale. The regiment was composed of a Car Company, three Tank Companies (two in Riga and one in Daugavpils), a Road Company, and an Instructor Company. armored trains, of which Latvia had two, were incorporated into a separate regiment after the war.

1st Cavalry Regiment, Daugavpils

The Daugavpils Cavalry Regiment was also formed in the days of the Independence War. In 1919-1920, at the peak of hostilities, Latvian liberal forces had six troops of cavalry. In the province of Kurzeme, the troop was based in Liepaja, in Vidzeme, Malnava, in Latgale, Malta, and in Zemgale, based in Daugavpils. Also there were the Latgale Geurilla Regiment, located in Jaunlatgale and the 13th Tukums Regiment located in Ludza. In 1921, all the separate troops and regiments were combined into one regiment located on Andrew Pumpurs Street in Daugavpils. The regiment consisted of 5 Squadrons. Eighteen Cavalrymen died in the fight for independence and a monument was unveiled to

Illustration 24: This group of officers appears to be watching a parade or demonstration. An Orthodox minister is seated in the foreground.

them in Daugavpils in 1923 with the inscription "The Spirit of Heroes Will Live Forever Among Us."

Latvia's Navy

Like most of the Latvian military, the Navy was founded during the tumult of the Independence War. Upon the inception of the Navy in the summer of 1919, seagoing forces were composed of requisitioned civilian vessels. Initially comprised of a coastal protection division and a small flotilla whose main mission was the destruction of underwater mines in the Daugava river, the vessels were returned to their owners and government-owned ships were comissioned after victory over Soviet forces in 1920.

Latvia's Navy was not initially a separate service, but rather a "Sea Coast Guard" Squadron under the Marine Department (later Naval Division) composed of seafaring elements of the 5th Cesis Infantry Regiment. Upon the defeat of Bolshevik forces in Riga in 1919, the mining ship "Red Latvia" (later renamed *Virsaitis* or "Chief") was

Illustration 25: The Latvian Navy's flagship Virsaitis (Chief). Originally a mine ship built for the German Kriegsmarine in 1917, the Virsaitis was sunk in Soviet service after striking a mine in the Gulf of Finland. The wreck of the Virsaitis was discovered in 2011.

surrendered to German marine forces along with thirteen smaller vessels which the Bolsheviks had seized, which were then returned to their owners.

When nationalist forces turned against their former allies, the German-composed West Russian Volunteer Army, the squadron played a crucial role in the control of the Daugava and participated actively in several battles during the war against Bermondtian forces.

Illustration 26: A medallion minted for Virsaitis' crew. The flagship appears to be fitted with a low frequency antenna on its mast.

Latvia's financial situation during the greater part of the first independence period did not allow for the maintanance of a Navy, but a Sea Coast Defence Squadron was maintained. In 1938, amidst rising tensions and conflict in Europe, the squadron was officially renamed the Latvian Navy and General Janis Balodis presented the Navy with its flag and motto "We Are United in Latvia's Holy Name."

The main Latvian naval port was in Liepaja, Kurzeme province but ports also existed in Ventspils and of course, Riga. In 1938, the Latvian Navy was made up of the two warships *Virsaitis* and *Varonis*, a mining wing, a submarine wing, and the 8th Naval Aviation Squadron, a fleet reconnaisance unit. The Navy numbered 590 seamen and 60 officers. The Navy was disbanded in 1940 by the occupation of Latvia by the Soviet Union.

Graphic: Structure of the Latvian Military 1920-1940

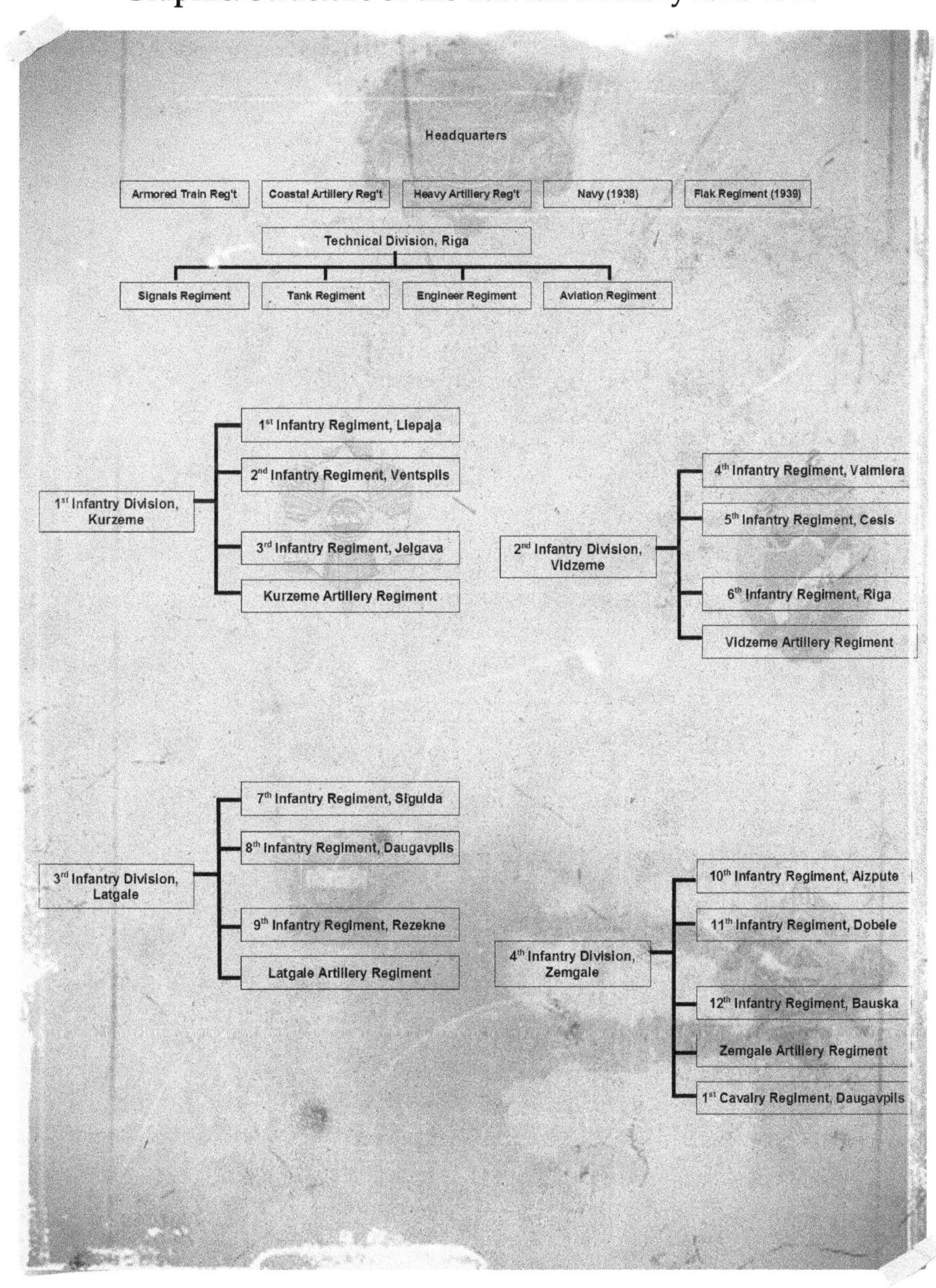

"Dressed in a soldier's greatcoat,
His helmet steel-grey,
His sword shining in the sun,
His horse magnificent, fast.
With music and with bravery,
The enemy will soon be defeated,
With music, songs, and victory,
They will ride back home again."

- "Goodbye Vidzeme," Janis Cimze (1814-1881)

IV - Weapons

In the early days of the Latvian army, the personal and section weapons used were diverse. Because, for the latter part of the Great War, the front lines literally split the country in two, weapons of both German and Russian manufacture were used. This of course posed problems for ammunition supply and the training of soldiers. Personal weapons included the Russian Mosin-Nagant series of rifles, mostly the Model 1891 rifle, and the German Mauser Model 1898 rifle.

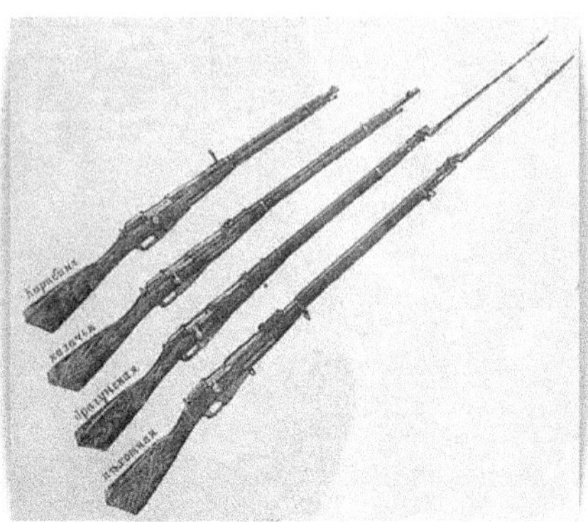

Illustration 27: 3-Line (Mosin Nagant) Series of Rifles.

Top to Bottom: 1907 Carbine, 1891 Cossack, Dragoon rifle, Standard 1891.

Illustration 28: Latvian soldiers form up with their English made Charger Loading Lee Enfield Rifles, a rifle made obsolete in British service by the advent of the SMLE rifle.

With Operation Red Trek, British arms were added to the mix of Russian and German. Initially, in early 1919, Great Britian supplied 50 machine guns and 5 000 rifles with ammunition to Latvian forces. In exchange for grain, France granted Latvia an 11 million Franc loan which Latvia used to buy 10 000 rifles, 550 machine guns, and 30 artillery pieces. In September 1919, Britain shipped an additional 20 000 rifles, 16 artillery pieces, 25 more machine guns, and 6 trucks. Still more supplies came in from England when another 18 000 rifles and additional guns were delivered along with some fighting vehicles in need of repairs. Pilsudski Jusefa, a Polish Marshal, sent Latvia 6 000 rifles and ammunition free of charge.

Ultimately, British weapons became the officially issued weapons of the Latvian military. This simplified logistics after the feat of fighting the Independence War where even identical caliber weapons needed separate and incompatible ammunition.

Illustration 29: An early photo of Latvian soldiers practicing marksmanship with German Gewehr 98 rifles. Note the Tsarist Russian clothing on some of the men.

Illustration 30: An enlisted man with webbing and ammunition pouches. His slash cuffs indicate this picture to be post 1929. He wears the later style French Adrian style helmet and his spurs and carbine indicate he belongs to the 1st Daugavpils Cavalry. The rifle is a Lee Enfield Mk II Carbine.

Rifles

There is a bit of confusion about the main infantry rifle of the Latvian army, some of which was caused by Latvian sources when they mis-dubbed the rifle they received in quantity from the British as the "Ross-Enfield." In fact, no such rifle exists.

There were two main infantry rifles supplied to the Latvians at the end of World War I in support of the civil war. These rifles included Canadian Ross rifles, a controversial indigenously designed and produced rifle capable of firing standard British .303" ammunition, and most often seen, the American built, British designed Pattern 14 rifle also chambered for standard British .303 ammunition. Although there are some photos of Latvians with Lee-Enfield rifles, neither the Ross nor the Pattern 14 (actually a modified Mauser design), had any relation to the British Lee-Enfield. The Pattern 14 rifle became the standard issue rifle of the Latvian interwar army.

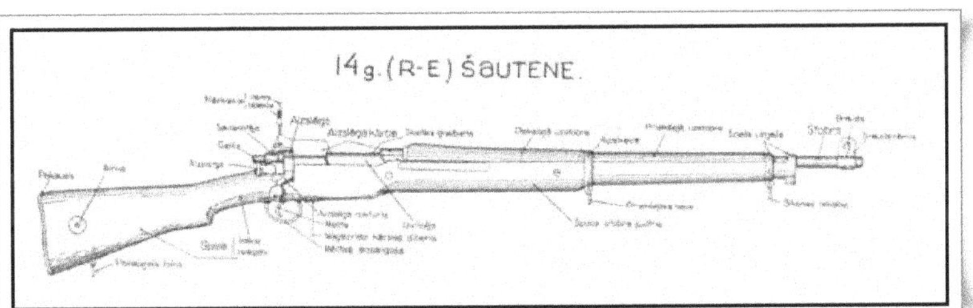

Illustration 31: A drawing of the Pattern 14 (P14) rifle from a Latvian Infantry manual, C. 1934.

The Pattern 14 rifle, manufactured by Remington and Winchester in the United States, was a stop-gap rifle produced to bolster the numbers of personal weapons available to the British Expeditionary Force in Europe at the outset of the Great War. Very few rifles were actually issued to troops, and they sat in British stores for most of the war.

The Pattern 14 was simpler to manufacture than the Lee-Enfield and had a Mauser-type action with integral box magazine holding 5 rounds of .303 caliber ammunition. The stock design also heavily

Illustration 32: A Latvian posing with a Pattern 14 Rifle and pre-1929 kepi hat. Note the British pattern cotton web sling.

borrowed from the Germans but had the distinctive English half-pistol grip and American style peep sights that would, in the future, be the standard for Western military rifles until the advent of universal optics.

It is reported that approximately 40 000 of these rifles were supplied to Latvians during the civil war period. More could have been purchased or otherwise aquired during independence.

Machine Guns

Machine guns, by any account the mainstay of a modern armed force, were also of British origin. Three main types of infantry support weapons were supplied by the British to the Latvians. Unlike the main infantry rifles, these guns were not cast-aways but valuable and advanced weapons intended to form the backbone of the Latvian army.

Illustration 33: Two soldiers posing with P14 rifles and fixed bayonets.

The Lewis Gun, a water-cooled machine gun of American design and British manufacture, was likely familiar to Latvians as it had been supplied to Imperial Russia before the revolution. Its distinctive pan magazine held up to 97 rounds of ammunition, which made it an ideal light support weapon for its time. The second type of machine gun provided to Latvia was the British version of the famous Maxim gun, the Vickers Machine Gun. The Vickers was also water-cooled with a large radiator on the barrel, but used non-disintegrating cloth or metal belts to feed ammunition. The Vickers was extremely reliable, but could take up to 6 men to operate if one includes the soldiers required to carry the bulky ammunition belts. The Vickers was also extremely heavy, weighing in at almost 50kg with water and tripod.

A Latvian diagram of the Vickers "heavy" machinegun on a British Mount.

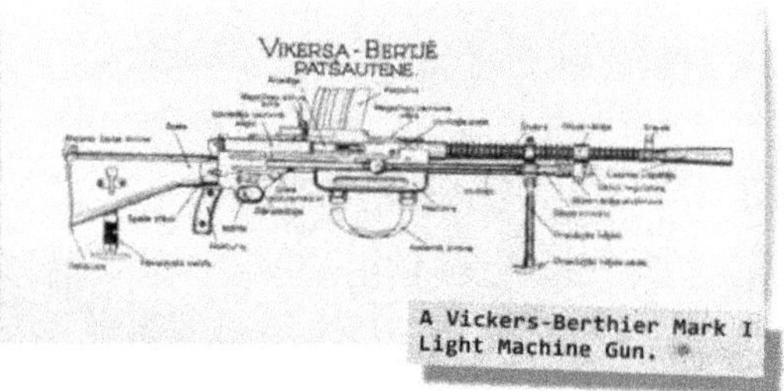

A Vickers-Berthier Mark I Light Machine Gun.

A Lewis Machine Gun with distinctive pan magazine.

A light machine gun was also supplied to the Latvians in the form of the Vickers-Berthier Mk. 1. The gun was purchased by the Latvian government after 1928 to facilitate the need for a light machine gun for fast infantry advances.

Often confused with the British BREN gun (which ultimately won the contract for production for the British army), the Vickers-Berthier had a similar looking top-mounted box magazine which held 30 rounds of .303 British ammunition.

Illustration 34: Circa 1920, two soldiers posing in field uniforms. The one on the right is holding a P14 rifle and has a white student batallion arm-band, the soldier on the left appears to have a hunting rifle.They both wear the round sunburst cap-badge.

Artillery

Latvian artillery presented much the same picture as its personal weapons. Russian, German, and English artillery pieces were common.

In terms of field artillery, gunners are often seen with Schneider M1897 77mm guns, Krupp 77mm guns, and even British Mk IV 18 Pounders.

Heavy artillery was provided by the Schneider M1913 105mm and 1910 152mm. Latvia also had a quantity of Russian M1910 107mm guns.

Anti-aircraft artillery consisted of Oerlikon 20mm cannons and the British Vickers 75mm AA gun. Anti-tank guns were Bohler 47mm and Bofors M35 37mm guns. 80mm mortors were normally used by mortor companies.

Illustration 35: Latvian soldiers firing a Russian model M1910 107mm artillery gun. Note the Russian M15 helmets.

Tanks

The Latvian armored regiment began with only four armored cars, two Putilov-Garford M1916 cars named *Kurzemnieks* and *Lacplesis* a Sheffield-Simplex named *Imants,* and an Austin armored Car named *Zemgalietis*.

Illustration 36: A Garford armored truck named Lacplesis, captured from the Russians, was taken out by German forces during battle in 1919.

In the summer of 1919, Latvian forces used both *Lacplesis* and *Zemgalietis* successfully in battle near Krustpils. In the fall, *Lacplesis, Kurzemnieks,* and *Imants* were influential in battles against the German Bermontian forces in Jelgava, Kalnciema, and Smarde Tukums damaging three German armored trains.

On November 8th, *Lacplesis* was taken out by German forces but Latvian forces gained two more cars named *Max* and *Moritz*. The small Latvian armored corps grew to 8 cars and participated in the Latgale battles which ultimately pushed communist forces back into Russia.

Illustration 37: British -made Mark B Tank

Illustration 38: The famous Mark V tank. Latvian tanks were hermaphrodite or "composite" models.

It was not until after the Independence War that Latvia created the Armored Vehicle Regiment. Latvia purchased several tanks, including Mark B and Mark V tanks from Great Britain which had formerly belonged to the Northwest Army.

In addition to English heavy Mark V and Mark B medium tanks, Latvia aquired a number of Fiat 3000 light assault tanks in the late 1920s from Italy. As a device to make war more mobile and overcome the quagmire of trench warfare, motorized armoured divisions were essential to any modern army.

The Latvian "Autotanku" regiment was subordinated to the Riga Technical Division and was headquartered in Latvia's capital. The First and Third Tank Company were also located in Riga, and the Second Tank Company was located in Daugavpils, close to the planned line of defence in the event of a Soviet Invasion.

In 1939, the regiment consisted of 35 officers, 274 instructors, and 515 men. Commanded by General Otto Grosbart, the 3 Tank Battalions each had 27 tanks, 6 armoured cars, 30 support vehicles, 1o passenger cars and 15 motor-cycles.

Tanks Were Allocated by Company:
1st Company - Mark V, Mark B, Fiat 3000
2nd Company - Vickers Tanks
3rd Company - Vickers Tanks

Aircraft

The Latvian Aviation Regiment's planes were varied and were mostly sourced from Britain, France, and Italy. One of the most notable achievements of the Independence period, however, was that Latvia managed to design and build its own series of training aircraft which rivaled the best technology available in Europe at the time.

Illustration 39: Latvian designed and manufactured VEF I-12

The state electrotechnical factory VEF, maker of the world-famous Minox camera, began producing Latvian training aircraft, with an eye to eventually make production fighters, in the late 1930s. It produced only

Illustration 40: A Hawker-Hind, showing the red thunder-cross, the roundel of the Latvian airforce, that was applied to all Latvian Aviation Regiment aircraft. Long before Nazism, the symbol was a popular design in military culture. The Latvian Student Battalion also had a thunder-cross on its flag.

a handful of VEF I-12, I-15, and I-17 aircraft, only to be stopped by the Soviet occupation in 1940.

Illustration 41: A Bristol Bulldog with British markings in RAF service. Latvia purchased twelve Bulldogs but sold eleven of them in 1937 (one had crashed) to Basque forces during the Spanish Civil War. By then they were nearing obsolescence.

The British designed and manufactured Gloster Gladiator was the most numerous fighter in the Latvian Air Regiment. After the sale of Latvia's eleven remaining Bristol Bulldogs to Spanish nationalist forces via a Czech agent in 1937, Latvia placed an order with Glouster of England for 26 Mark I aircraft. Armed with four Vickers Mark VM 7.7mm machine guns, the aircraft, along with three Hawker-Hind bombers, were acquired for the sum of £120,000 (about 10 million 2010 US Dollars) and raised by public lottery and from the sale of the Bulldogs.

Sometime between August and November 1937, the Gladiators were delivered by sea to Riga. They were serialized in two ranges: from 114 to 126, and 163 to 175. Following testing they were divided into two fighter squadrons both based in Riga. In 1938, Fighter Squadron 123 and

124 were stood up. After the Soviet invasion in 1941, the Air Regiment's aircraft were assumed by the Soviet Union who repainted them in Soviet Airforce colors, however, the German advance in 1942 was so rapid that a number of aircraft formerly belonging to the Latvian Air Regiment were captured by the Germans.

Illustration 42: Numbering 26 in total, the Gloster Gladiator was the main fighter aircraft of the Latvian army between the wars.

The Latvian Aviation Regiment in Numbers

Aircraft Model	Producing Country	Number Purchased	Year Acquired
Fighter Aircraft (65)			
Gloster Gladiator I	Great Britain	26	1937
Ansaldo A-1 Ballila	Italy	12	1923
Bristol Bulldog II	Great Britain	12	1929
Martinsyde ADC-1	Great Britain	7	1926
Fiat CR-1	Italy	6	1927
Gourdou Lesseure B3	France	1	1924
Martinsyde F-4 Buzzard	Great Britain	1	1924
Reconnaissance Aircraft (46)			
Letow-Smolik S-16	Czechoslovakia	21	1927
Stampe et Vertongen SV5	Belgium	11	1935
De Haviland DH-9A	Great Britain	7	1926
PHA-10	Italy	4	1923
Hawker Hind B	Great Britain	3	1938
Training Aircraft (15)			
VEF I-17	Latvia	6	1940
Avro 548 N	Great Britain	2	1925
Avro 504 K	Great Britain	2	1925
VEF I-12	Latvia	2	1937
VEF I-15	Latvia	2	1939
Miles Magister	Great Britain	1	1939
Maritime Aircraft (22)		**22**	
Heinkel He-4	Sweden	6	1926
Fairey SAEL	Great Britain	4	1934
Savoia S-16 ICB	Italy	3	1923
Hanriot H17	France	2	1924
Hansa Brandenburg	Finland	2	1927
Caudron C60	France	1	1925
Link-Svenska-Pirat	Sweden	1	1929

Warships and Other Naval Vessels

Latvia had two main warships during the first independence: *Virsaitis*, a 525-ton-displacement mine-laying ship, armed with 30 mines, 75 and 57mm guns, and employing 70 sailors, and *Varonis*, a submarine service ship about half the size of the flagship.

Illustration 43: The mining ship Imants pictured in Soviet Russian captivity.

Virsaitis, although technically a mine-laying ship, was labeled as the "Ministry of War Guard Ship" and later simply as a "Warship." *Virsaitis* was captured by the Soviet Navy in 1941 after the occupation of Latvia. It was sunk during the Red Navy's evacuation of the Hanko peninsula during the Continuation War with Finland when it struck a mine. The wreck was discovered in 2011. *Varonis* also struck a mine and sank while in Soviet captivity.

Other mining ships included *Imants* and *Viesturs*. For the sum of six and a half million Lats, Latvia also purchased two new submarines from France, named *Ronis* and *Spidola*, both of which were delivered in 1927. Captured when the USSR occupied Latvia in 1940, both submarines were sunk in Soviet service when the German Navy blocked the port of Liepaja in 1941.

***"Greetings to the arisen hero.
Greetings to you, descendants of
the great hero Lacplesis,
You - Latvian Bear-Slayers."***

- 1922, Janis Čakste, Latvian President,
speech during the ceremony
awarding the Order of the Bear-Slayer

V – Uniforms and Insignia

The military had played a crucial role in developing the symbols of the nascent Latvian state. The Latvian Riflemen of the Russian Imperial army had even designed the state's flag in the First World War. Like the military apparatus itself, the insignia and unforms of the interwar Latvian army emerged out of the distinct units of Latvian Riflemen. From the unique cap badges to rank insignia, uniforms maintained some of the Imperial Russian design and layout but became quite different in appearance overall. They combined both German and Russian patterns and added unique Latvian elements.

Illustration 44: A Latvian artilleryman wearing the Imperial Russian trench cap and Russian pullover tunic.

Headdress

The standard cap badge, or cockade, was worn on virtually all Latvian military headdresses. It evolved from the badge of the Latvian Riflemen during World War One which consisted of a stylized sunburst, sword, a ring of oakleaves, all below a Russian imperial eagle. Initially, only the eagle was deleted, but later a new sunburst design was authorized and was worn on virtually every soldier's cap.

The Latvian coat of arms, depicting double gryphons and lions, a sunrise, and three stars representing the three Latvian provinces, was worn in conjunction with the finalized sunburst cockade on soft trench caps. This cockade is often described as an officer's cap badge because of its ornate design, but while it is a magnificent large badge made of bronze, it is seen equally as often on the enlisted ranks' caps as officers' caps in photographs.

Early caps of the Latvian army were merely Imperial Russian trench caps with either the Latvian Riflemen cockade (with imperial eagle deleted) or the early style sunburst cockade. A Latvian version of the trench cap was developed and is identified by its higher straight sides. There were three main types of Latvian-designed uniform *kepi*, or caps. The stiff-peaked 1923-1929 cap, on which only the sunburst cockade was worn, the post-1929 soft trench cap, on which both the coat of arms and sunburst cap badge were worn, and the *pilotka*, on which the sunburst cockade was worn. Both the early stiff cap and later soft cap had branch-colored fabric bands around the perimeter. The *pilotka* (in Russian), or pilot's cap, which became standard both in the Latvian military and the Soviet Russian military, was a wedge-shaped hat initially intended to be worn under a helmet. Popularized by pilots in the First World War, the *Pilotka* was issued in two colors in the Latvian military: the M1932 Kakhi color to match the Kakhi pullover tunic, and the standard dark green. A cold-weather version of the *pilotka* was also developed and issued. Worn with the wool great-coat, the cold-weather field hat had folding fur-lined ear-flaps that could be tied in the up or down positions.

Illustration 45: The coat of arms cockade, worn below the sunburst badge.

Illustration 46: The finalized standard cockade of the independence period.

Illustration 47: Pictured left, an enlisted man wears the 1923-1929 stiff-peaked cap with sunburst cockade. He also wears the insignia of the 4th Valmiera Infantry Regiment. The officer version of this hat had a double cord with the top one looped above the cockade instead of the chinstrap pictured here. The Corporal (center) wears the cherry-red infantry collar patches and the standard Latvian pilotka. Pictured right, this artillery gunner from the Latgale Artillery Regiment wears the post-1929 soft trench cap with both the coat of arms cockade and the sunburst cockade above.

Illustration 48: A photo dated 1933 - Latvian soldiers pose in field caps. A Russian M15 helmet is pictured between the two soldiers in the front row. One soldier is wearing the noticably lighter late khaki colored tunic.

Combat helmets were at first either Russian M15 Adrian pattern or German M16 helmets. In the mid 1920s, French style Adrian helmets were adopted, painted khaki with an "L" and three stars on the front.

Illustration 49: Soldiers from 4th Infantry Regiment (Valmiera) with Pattern 14 rifles and M16 helmets.They all wear the M1932 summer pullover tunic.

Illustration 51: A tank crew from the Armored Vehicle Regiment. They wear specialized helmets used specifically for confined areas.

Illustration 50: Three soldiers pose in great-coats and post-1929 caps.

Tunics and Coats

Illustration 52: This enlisted man is wearing a soft trench cap with both cockades, the standard garrison tunic, and cherry-red infantry collar patches.

As with headdress, Latvian tunics and trousers were initially modified Imperial Russian uniforms; some German uniforms were also utilized but generally anything that was available was used during the Independence War period.

Early uniforms were field gray, later changed to a dark greenish khaki color. The Russian-style pullover tunic was retained for field use, issued as the model M1932 tunic, and a button-up field tunic was also made in addition to the more formal garrison or dress tunic. A greatcoat was issued for winter dress, double-breasted for officers, single-breasted for the men.

Illustration 53: A soldier posing in the standard cold-weather wool greatcoat.

Illustration 54: This artilleryman wears the standard wool greatcoat and has a P14 rifle slung across his back.

The standard garrison tunic, seen most often in formal photographs, was wool or cotton with a high mandarin collar. Both large closure buttons and small epaullette, cuff, and pocket buttons (yellow for combat arms, white for administration) had the Latvian suburst symbol in relief. Officer's tunics and non-comissioned ranks tunics sported three pointed pocket flaps and French cuffs.

In 1929, the jacket was altered with slash cuffs instead of French cuffs. Piping, which is often seen in formal photos, was used to indicate branch with distinctive colors. Soldiers of the Armored Vehicle Regiment, for example, had red piping on a black uniform, while the Aviation Regiment had blue piping on a black uniform. Also, a light and heavy tunic were issued for summer and winter.

Illustration 55: An example of a Serzants (Seargant) marked tunic from the first independence period with details of the shoulder epaullette, showing 5th Infantry Regiment (Cesis) flashes, the rank tabs, and early French cuffs. The tunic buttons each have the sunburst symbol in relief with three stars representing the three administrative disctricts of Latvia. This particular tunic is pinned with a machine-gunner's badge.

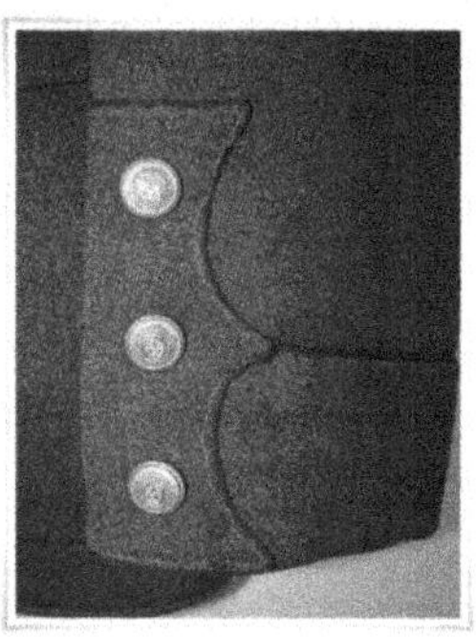

Illustration 56: An enlisted man posed in a post-1929 tunic. Note the straight-cut breast pockets.

Illustration 57: A Lance-Corporal and Private pose for a photo. The one on the left wears the M1932 Infantry Summer pullover tunic with 2nd Ventspils Regiment badge and machinegun and marksman proficiency badges. The man on the right wears the standard field tunic.

Illustration 58: A garrison tunic without insignia or badges. Also missing epaulettes, this tunic may have been modified in the Second World War.

Illustration 59: A Lieutenant's uniform with pistol and stiff-peaked hat (left) and enlisted man's uniform with M16 helmet and greatcoat (right). The rifle is a Mosin Nagant 1891.

Illustration 60: Soldiers posing in field uniforms, most of which are the M1932 Khaki color.

Navy Uniforms

Latvian Navy working uniforms followed the standard pattern established by the imperial navies at the time, particularly the British Royal Navy and Russian Navy. Included was the traditional naval cap as had been used in the Russian navy since 1811 with black silk ribbon bearing the name of the sailor's ship. A Latvian sunburst type cap badge also adorned the hat. Most notably, the striped undershirt, or *telnyashka* (in Russian), a salient symbol of the Russian and Soviet navies including special forces and marines, was used. The shirt had historically been used by civilian fisherman and merchants in Brittany and later the French Navy.

Illustration 61: A Sailor belonging to the Flagship Virsaitis

Rank Markings and Structure

Illustration 62: This photo shows a member of the Štāba Bataljons, or Staff Battalion, the headquarters of the Latvian army. Located in Riga, its members wore the distinctive light blue backed collar patches with blue piping along with the unique badge of the battalion on their epaullettes (post-1929).

Latvian ranks were displayed on collar tabs, just as in National Socialist era Germany and Soviet era Russia. Shoulder epaulettes, traditionally the place to display rank in the Russian empire, showed branch and regimental insignia instead. Gold numbers 1 to 12 indicated an infantry regiment, while artillery was represented by a letter, and other specialized regiments were indicated with unique badges.

Officers rank tabs had a diagonal bar embroidered out of gold silk. The patch was, in in the later independence period, colored appropriately to branch and featured gold metal (or white for non-combat arms) four or five point stars (and gold embroidered circle for Senior Lieutenant).

Non-Comissioned Officers had a white wool diagonal line from corner to corner of the tab on a branch-colored patch with gold metal stars and gold lace bars for Warrant Officer (or Master Sergeant - *Visserzants*) and above; yellow cloth bars were used for Sergeant, Corporal, and Lance-Corporal. Privates simply had a white wool line on a branch-colored patch.

Rank Insignia

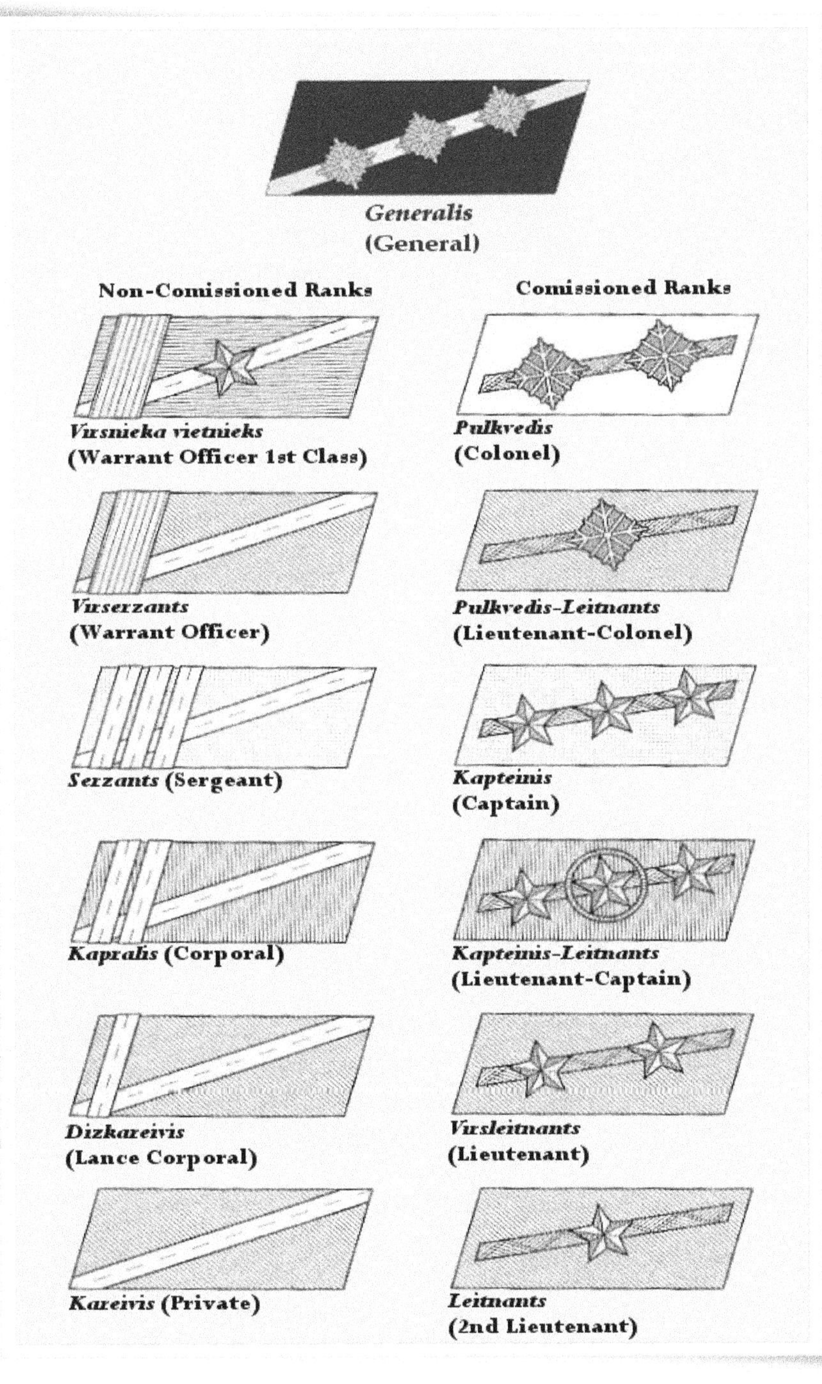

Uniform Piping and Collar-Patch Branch Colors (from 1931)

Branch of Service	Piping Color	Collar-Patches
General Staff, Headquarters	Light Blue	Light Blue
Divisional Staff, Infantry Regiments	Cherry Red	Cherry Red
Artillery Regiments	Blue	Blue
Cavalry Regiment	Orange	Orange
Signals and Engineer Regiments	Orange	Cherry Red
Armored Regiment	Cherry Red	Cherry Red
Supply	Blue	Black
Air Regiment	Blue	Cherry Red

Proficiency Badges

Worn on the tunic above the left breast pocket, proficiency badges indicated a soldier's competence with specific small arms. Badges were issued for the Maxim Heavy Machine Gun, Lewis Gun, Pattern 14 Rifle, and service pistol.

Illustration 63: All four proficiency badges (from top): Heavy Machine Gun, Light Machine Gun, Rifle, and Pistol.

Ceremonial Swords

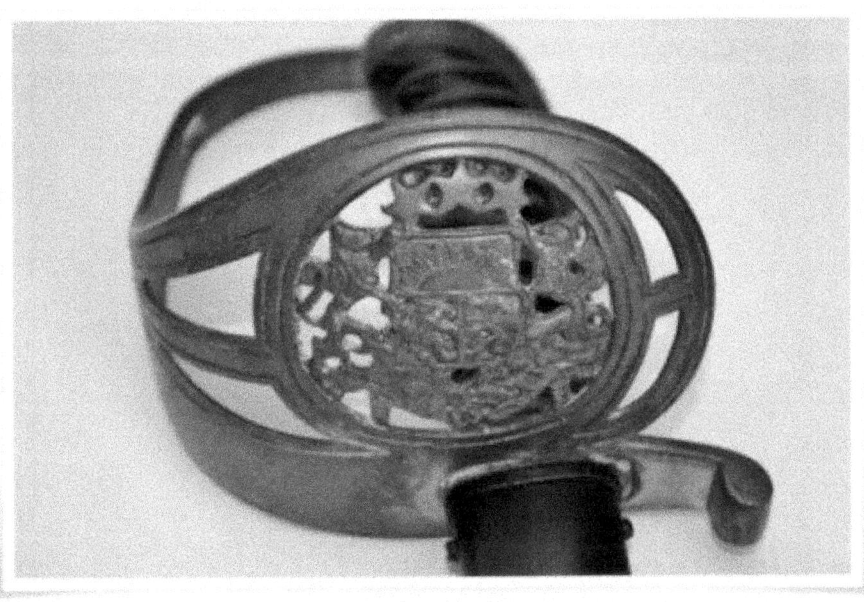

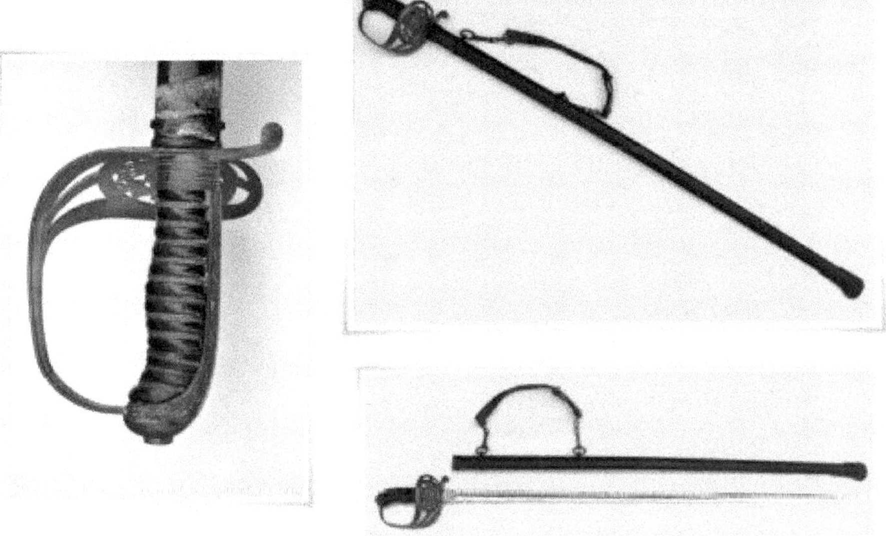

Illustration 64: Long abandoned as weapons of war, swords served only a symbolic and ceremonial role in the modern military. This Latvian officer's sword, made by E.&F. Horster of Solingen, Germany, features an ornate coat of arms on the cross-guard.

Illustration 65: Soldiers posing outside barracks of the former imperial military academy in Liepaja. The "K" on their shoulder epaullettes indicates they are light field artillery soldiers of the "Kurzemes Artilērijas Pulks" (Kurzeme Artillery Regiment) based in Liepaja. The photo is marked "4 Battery."

Illustration 66: This soldier wears the soft trench cap with the coat-of-arms insignia and starburst badge. His collar tabs identify him as a Lance-Corporal and his "D" shoulder insignia and breast badge identify him as a member of the Coastal Artillery Regiment based in Riga's Daugavgrivas Fortress.

Illustration 67: Another artilleryman from Riga's Coastal Artillery Regiment. Note the braided aguilette, letter "D" on his epaulettes, and distinctive breast-badge.

Illustration 68: Two enlisted men wearing pilotka caps, one with a dress tunic (left) and one with a field tunic (right). The ropes tied from their epaulettes, called aiguillettes, along with the breast-badge on the man pictured right, identify them as artillerymen.

Illustration 69: A mounted artillery soldier wearing the aiguillette, dress tunic, and stiff peaked dress cap.

Illustration 70: Jelgava 1940 - This photo shows a supply soldier mounted on horseback. The photo is inscribed: "Training a new team."

Illustration 71: A Lance-Corporal with pilotka and round cap badge. Marked Daugavpils and dated 1938.

Illustration 72: An unposed photo showing Latvian soldiers in greatcoats.

Illustration 73: Men digging fortifications. The soldier in the center is wearing an M16 helmet.

Breast Badges

Illustration 74: The Latvian Riflemen breast badge (left) and Red Latvian Riflemen breast badge (right). Note the only significant change was the removal of the imperial eagle and substitution of the communist star with hammer.

Breast-badges were one of the few permitted indicators of Latvian origin on the uniforms of the Russian Imperial Army. The original breast-badges of the Latvian riflemen were inscribed with the acronym in Latin script LSB for *Latviešu Strēlnieki Bataljons* (ПСБ in Cyrillic) with a stylized sunburst and oak-wreath crowned by a Russian imperial double-headed eagle. In the interwar Latvian Army, breast badges were used to indicate a soldier's regimental affiliation. So-named because they were worn on the left breast pocket of the tunic, these badges were jewellery-quality, ornate pieces of art that depicted historical symbols important to each regiment and often the founding date, usually a date from the Independence War that made Latvia a state.

There are dozens of these breast badges, each with major and minor variations. A book could be written about breast badges alone, and indeed it has been. In 2011, Janis Vigups *et al* published *Breast Badges of the Latvian Army 1918-1940* which contains nearly 500 pages of detail on these military artworks.

Featured here is by no means a complete compendium of breast badges but only some of the most common and important badges seen on Latvian soldiers in the independence period. For more detail, consult the abovementioned book.

Illustration 75: An Imperial Period officer's breast-badge.

There were 12 Infantry Regiments in the interwar Latvian army, each with its own symbols and history. Most of the regiments were instrumental in some way to the winning of independence in the tumult of the 1919-1921 period. In the badges, one can see the prominence of the swastika or thunder-cross in Latvian military culture. Such symbols can look ominous now, but before the rise of the Nazi regime in Germany, the symbol had no racial connotation or connection to fascism. Other pagan symbols abound, and in the badges one can sense the blending of Latvian cluture and symbolism with its pre-christian past. This symbolism referenced a rejection of German rule which began in 1201 as well as Latvia's newfound independence from Imperial Russia.

Infantry Badges

1st Regiment, Liepaja

2nd Regiment, Ventspils

3rd Regiment, Jelgava

4th Regiment, Valmiera

5th Regiment, Cesis

6th Regiment, Riga

7th Regiment, Sigulda

8th Regiment, Daugavpils

9th Regiment, Rezekne

10th Regiment, Aizpute

11th Regiment, Dobele

12th Regiment, Bauska

Illustration 76: A Latvian soldier posed for a photo in dress uniform. His collar patches are backed with artillery blue. He wears the Heavy Artillery regimental badge on his left breast.

Illustration 77: The Heavy Artillery (Smagās Artilērijas Pulks) regimental badge, pictured above and left, features the founding date of 26 May, 1921.

Artillery Regiments

Kurzeme Regiment

Zemgale Regiment

Heavy Artillery

Vidzeme Regiment

Coastal Artillery

Latgale Regiment

Special Regiments

Armored Train Regiment

Armored Vehicle Regiment

1st Cavalry Regiment

Aviation Regiment

Electrotechnical Division

1st Engineers Regiment

Military Orders / Decorations

Latvia had three main state orders during the independence period. These orders were awarded for military merit, as honors for foreign dignitaries, and as recognition for accomplished civil servants. Other awards and orders were developed but awarded only for a very short time before the Soviet occupation.

Illustration 78: Order of Lacplesis (the Bear-Slayer). Established 1919. Stylized swastika with crossed swords. Lacplesis is pictured in the center.

Order of the Bear-Slayer

Latvia's highest honor was the Order of the Bear-Slayer. The Bear-Slayer was a 19th century nationalist myth that came to occupy a central position in state imagery in Latvia during the 1918-1940 period. The order was awarded mainly to participants in the War of Independence but also select foreign soldiers or political leaders the most famous, or infamous of which, was Italian dictator Bennito Mussolini. King Albert of Belgium was also awarded the order, along with two French Generals, an Estonian General, and a Polish Marshal. The order had three classes, and out of only eleven first-class orders made, nine were actually awarded.

Order of the Three Stars

Illustration 79: Order of the Three Stars, 2nd Class.

The Order of the Three Stars, Medal of Honor (*Triju Zvaigžnu Ordenis, goda zime*) also had three classes. Established in 1924, it was mostly awarded for civil service, however, not as a military decoration, although military leaders had received it when filling a civil office, such as the Swedish King.

Illustration 81: Order of the Three Stars, 3rd Class.

Illustration 80: Order of the Three Stars, 1st Class.

Viesturs Order

The Viesturs order, named after King Viesturs who resisted German occupation in the 13th century, was awarded "in recognition of accomplishments in the training, development and upgrading of the national armed forces; in the safeguarding and strengthening of the state's security and social order; in the defence of the state's frontiers; and in the promotion of an enhanced sense of national patriotism."

Illustration 82: Viesturs Order

"The other Latvian warriors all,
His kin and brethren, countrymen,
Soon, one by one, were doomed to fall,
By stronger forces conquered then.

The Strangers came into their place
And as harsh masters ruled the folk.
Bear-Slayer's folk, his well-loved race,
For ages long bore slavery's yoke."

- The Bear-Slayer, Andrejs Pumpurs, (1841-1902)

VI – The End of an Era

The Latvian military of the interwar period met its end in 1940 when the Soviet Union occupied Latvia without a fight. Finland, on the other hand, had refused to cooperate with Soviet demands, and as a consequence a bloody war ensued costly to both sides. Eventually, Finland won its freedom for this sacrifice, but elements of geography played to its advantage. In the Baltics, well-trained and well-equipped soldiers were ordered not to fight as their nation was occupied by one of the bloodiest regimes in history.

Illustration 83: One of the few symbols of Latvia allowed on Waffen SS uniforms during World War II

Litene Massacre

In Krape, a small rural village in the district of Latvia's capital Riga, there worked a small compliment of exiles: former officers of the Polish army who fled German atrocities in their homeland. The men worked at the nearby sawmill and a few surrounding farms and in their off time they gathered in the village center and played volleyball and soccer with the locals.

In the spring of 1940, Karpe's Polish guests suddenly vanished. The NKVD had sent trucks in the night and collected the men for transport. They were taken to a forest near the small village of Katyn near the border between Russia and Belarus and murdered as part of a larger massacre of Polish "undersirables."

The 1940 mass killing of 22,000 Polish officers known as the Katyn Massacre formed the template for Soviet atrocities in its occupied territories. Massacres of army officers, public officials, and entire families were repeated throughout the Soviet Union. It was no wonder that at the end of the Second World War, citizens of the Soviet Union were the only Europeans to flee from their own liberating army.

Illustration 84: Latvian deportees board a train in 1941.Many would die before reaching their destination.

The Soviet occupation of Latvia in 1941 was characterized by mass arrests and deportations, part of a larger scheme of social and ethnic cleansing by the Soviet Union taking place throughout its newly aquired territories and remembered as "the year of terror." The NKVD planned the massacre and deportation of 1,100 Latvian army officers to coincide with extra-judicial deportations of approximately 15,500 civilians, including some 2,400 children on 14

Illustration 85: Mass grave at Litene as it appeared in 1991.

June, 1941.

Following the occupation, the Latvian army was re-designated the 24th Territorial Corps of the Red Army. In the spring of 1941, most officers were sent to the Latvian army's summer training camp at Litene in the province of Vidzeme. While on an alleged training mission, the officers were arrested. 200 officers were massacred at Litene and interred in a mass grave. 80 officers were killed in Riga and 560 were deported to Norilsk, Siberia, where they were sentenced to death or hard labor. Only 90 officers ever returned to Latvia from Siberia.

German Occupation

The quick advance of German forces in July 1941 meant that the remainder of the Latvian army, now the 24th Territorial Corps, was ordered to evacuate to Soviet Russia. Some soldiers deserted and remained behind in their homeland.

Illustration 86: A recruiting poster from World War II for German forces. The picture shows a soldier dressed in a Latvian army greatcoat with a Russian Mosin Nagant rifle.

While Latvians hoped things might be better under German occupation, the reality was bleak. The remains of the Latvian army and all national symbols were ruthlessly suppressed under the new occupation. As the war turned against Germany, and the administration began to realize that the inhabitants of the occupied *Ostland* may be their last hope, Latvian symbols, uniforms, and insignia made a comeback with many soldiers in the service of Germany wearing Latvian army issue kit and equipment. In 1943, the Latvian Legion was created as a conscript army and took the form of two *Waffen SS* Divisions. Latvian uniforms were relegated to rear echelon use, with SS uniforms, unfortunately, forming the image of many Latvians in the war. This image would be a propaganda boon for the Soviet regime after the war ended as it claimed, falsely, that Latvians who resisted Soviet re-occupation were fascists.

Illustration 87: Two Worlds: Latvians observe Nazi propaganda comparing Soviet "subhumans" and the German "master race" after the Germans occupy Riga in 1941. Source: Das Bundesarchiv.

A New National Army in the Forests

The Independence Period was brought to a definite and, as many thought, permanent end in 1945, when the Soviet Union took control of

Latvia again. Expecting the Soviets to honor the Riga Peace Treaty of 1920 and the allies to honor the Atlantic Charter, and unaware of the secret protocols of the Molotov-Ribbentrop Pact, Latvians were instead left under Soviet rule at the Yalta Conference in 1945.

Illustration 88: A meeting of Forest Brothers in the forests of Usma, Kurland, 1946. The photo was taken by NKVD agent M. Vitolins. Most partisan groups were infiltrated by Soviet agents before members could be killed or arrested.

The people of the Baltics including Latvia, refused to accept the fate assigned to them by the great powers. The last place Latvian national army symbols and uniforms were ultimately seen were in the forests of the Latvian countryside. Dressed in a mixture of civilian clothing, Red Army, German, and interwar national army uniforms, these men, known as "Forest-Brothers," coordinated their efforts to again push Soviet forces back into Russia as they had in 1919. The Forest Brothers existed by virtue of a broad base of local support and did not receive the Western assistance their forebears did at the end of World War I. Instead, they fought a war in the woods until finally being defeated by betrayal, secret police infiltration, and waves of Soviet ethnic cleansing in the early 1950s.

Return of the Latvian National Army

The Latvian military was reborn in 1991 when the Soviet Union suddenly and unexpectedly collapsed. Many elements of the pre-war era were brought back – even dress unforms in the Latvian military today recall the look of those soldiers of the 1920s and 30s. Latvia, now a member of the EU and NATO, is showing again its Western orientation and aspirations.

Illustration 89: Changing of the guard at the Freedom Monument in Riga, July 2001. Latvian ceremonial uniforms are reminiscent of the uniforms of the first independence.

Contact the Author:

To make this publication as complete and accurate as possible, I welcome your suggestions and corrections. Please contact me at historybooks@hotmail.ca

Other Books by this Author

Bear-Slayers: Latvian Myth, Memory, and the World Wars

www.ingramcontent.com/pod-product-compliance
Ingram Content Group UK Ltd.
Pitfield, Milton Keynes, MK11 3LW, UK
UKHW051128260726
13967UKWH00010B/2931

9 781300 015918